BESTSELLING NON-FI

- Annihilation of Caste by Dr B.R. Ambedkar
  Social Science, ISBN: 9789390492732

- Believe in Yourself by Joseph Murphy
  Self-Help/Motivational, ISBN: 9789388118385

- How I Made $2,000,000 in the Stock Market by Nicolas Darvas
  Self-Help, ISBN: 9789389716283

- How to Attract Money by Joseph Murphy
  Self-Help, ISBN: 9789388118408

- How to Enjoy Your Life and Your Job by Dale Carnegie
  Self-Help, ISBN: 9789387669017

- How to Stop Worrying and Start Living by Dale Carnegie
  Self-Help, ISBN: 9789380914817

- How to Win Friends and Influence People by Dale Carnegie
  Self-Help, ISBN: 9788180320217

- Jail Diary and Other Writings by Bhagat Singh
  Biographies & Memoirs, ISBN: 9789390492398

- Know Your Worth by NK Sondhi & Vibha Malhotra
  Self-Help/Motivational, ISBN: 9788180320231

- Meditations by Marcus Aurelius
  Philosophy, ISBN: 9789388118736

- My Experiments with Truth by Mahatma Gandhi
  Biographies & Memoirs, ISBN: 9789387669291

- My Inventions: The Autobiography of Nikola Tesla
  Biographies & Memoirs, ISBN: 9789388118132

Search the book by its ISBN

BESTSELLING NON-FICTION

- Relativity by Albert Einstein
  Science/Physics, ISBN: 9789380914220

- Reminiscences of a Stock Operator by Edwin Lefevre
  Business/Stock Market, ISBN: 9788194764816

- Success Through a Positive Mental Attitude by Napoleon Hill
  Self-Help, ISBN: 9789390492435

- The Art of War by Sun Tzu
  Self-Help, ISBN: 9789380914893

- The Autobiography of a Yogi by Paramahansa Yogananda
  Biographies & Memoirs, ISBN: 9789380914602

- The Diary of a Young Girl by Anne Frank
  Biographies & Memoirs, ISBN: 9789380914312

- The Elements of Style by William Strunk
  Non-Fiction, ISBN: 9789389157123

- The Law of Success by Napoleon Hill
  Self-Help, ISBN: 9788180320927

- The Power of Your Subconscious Mind by Joseph Murphy
  Self-Help, ISBN: 9788180320958

- The Richest Man in Babylon by George S. Clason
  Business & Economics, ISBN: 9789387669369

- The Science of Getting Rich by Wallace D. Wattles
  Self-Help, ISBN: 9788180320972

- The World as I See It by Albert Einstein
  Non-Fiction, ISBN: 9789388118125

Search the book by its ISBN

51 Must Know Facts About BRAIN

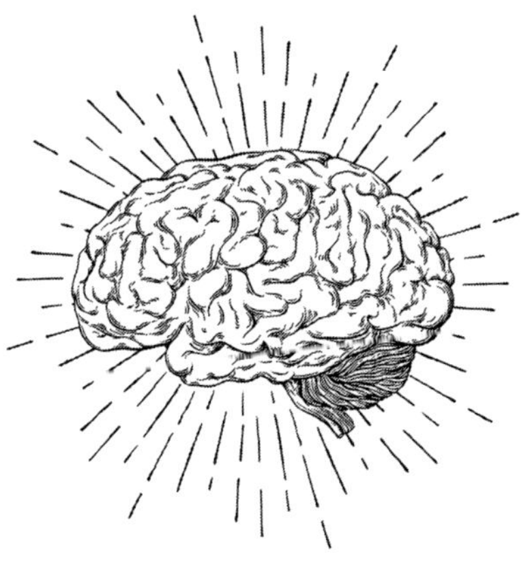

GENERAL PRESS

Published by

GENERAL PRESS

4805/24, Fourth Floor, Krishna House
Ansari Road, Daryaganj, New Delhi - 110002
Ph : 011-23282971, 45795759
E-mail : generalpressindia@gmail.com

www.generalpress.in

First Edition : 2023

ISBN : 9789354994371

Published by Azeem Ahmad Khan for General Press

Contents

Introduction 7

51 Must Know Facts About Brain. 11-76

Introduction

The human brain is extraordinary. It is the body's control centre. We must know how neurons work, how the brain develops, how it controls movement and perceives the senses, what happens during sleep, and how language, learning, and memory are developed. Technology is finally unlocking the secrets of the brain. It is explaining why we behave the way we do. It is helping experts develop new methods and machines to boost our brain power and it is revealing the unique capabilities we all have inside our heads.

The human brain is the command centre for the human nervous system. It receives signals from the body's sensory organs and outputs information to the muscles. The human brain has the same basic structure as other mammal brains but is larger in relation to body size than any other brains.

There are about 100 billion tiny cells in your brain called 'neurons'. There are so many that it would take you over 3,000 years to count them all. Around 77% of your brain is just water and it stops growing when you are around 25, but that doesn't mean that you have reached your intellectual peak. The adult human brain weighs about 3 pounds (1,350g). It is about 2% of the total body weight and it is the last part of your body to die.

Lively and information-packed, '51 Must Know Facts about Brain' is a must read for you to know each and every important fact about the brain.

51

MUST KNOW FACTS ABOUT BRAIN

1

The largest section is the cerebrum and it makes up over ¾ of the brain's volume. It consists of neurons and nerve fibers that transmit information from the neurons throughout the brain and the body. The cerebrum controls the higher functions such as learning, reasoning and speech, plus senses like sight and hearing.

2

The brain is not only the most complex organ in the human body; it is the most complex structure in the known universe. As part of the nervous system, the brain coordinates with all of the body's functions.

3

The brain is comprised of four main regions—the cerebrum, the cerebellum, the brainstem and the diencephalon. Each one controls specific tasks. They work in sync to ensure that the bodily functions are fully operational.

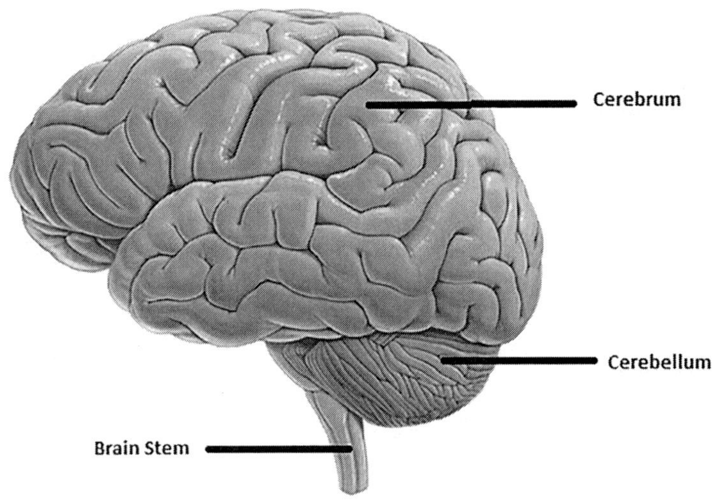

Cerebrum
Cerebellum
Brain Stem

4

Under the cerebrum, is the second largest part of the brain called the cerebellum. Much like the cerebrum, the cerebellum has nerve cells and nerve fibers. It carries signals to the other parts of the brain and the spinal cord. The cerebellum is responsible for carrying muscle movements; particularly those that help maintain the body's balance and posture.

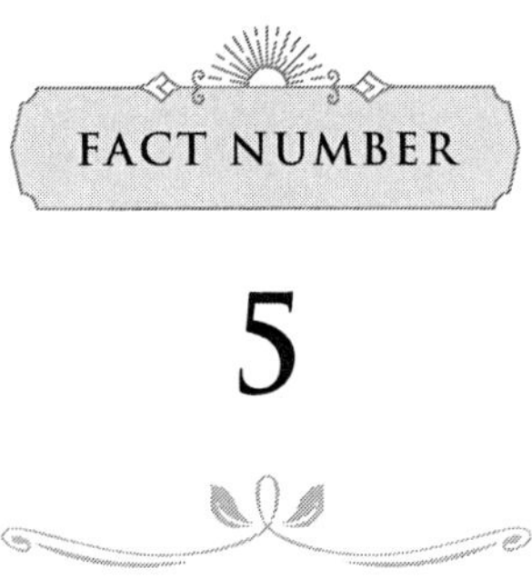

5

The third region of the brain is the brainstem. It lies in front of the cerebellum and anchors the brain to the spinal cord. The brainstem is the collection of structures that include the pons—a massive nerve fibers that carries sensory information, the midbrain—region of fibers and structures that help control movement along with auditory and visual processing and the medulla oblongata—which creates motor and sensory pathways between the midbrain, the pons and the spinal cord. Altogether, the parts of the brainstem control the vital bodily functions, such as cardiac activity, respiration, digestion and sleep.

6

The fourth region is located above the brainstem and makes up the core of the brain—the diencephalon. About the size of an apricot, the diencephalon is a grouping of several structures—the thalamus, which processes and transmit information from all senses except smell, and the hypothalamus and pituitary glands, which work together to produce and regulate neurochemicals. These structures help govern sensations, weight regulation, energy and instinctual behaviours.

7

The brain has even evolved mechanisms to protect itself. One such mechanism is the blood-brain barrier, a semipermeable, cellular wall, that only allows specific chemicals to enter from the body's bloodstream into the brain. Despite this protection, tumours and other complications can lead to life threatening problems and diseases in the brain, such as dementia. Thankfully, scientists have found ways to improve brain health. Staying physically active and eating a balanced diet may preserve cognitive functions and even reduce the risk of developing alzimiers.

8

The brain floats in a bath of a clear liquid called cerebral spinal fluid, which acts as a shock absorber. The brain produces half the cup of this fluid everyday!

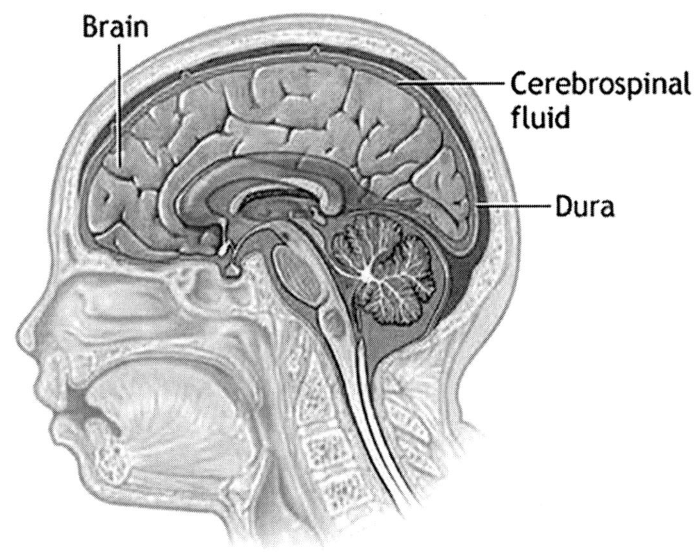

Brain
Cerebrospinal
fluid
Dura

9

The brain is surrounded by twenty-two bones, which make up the cranium—the fancy science word for the skull. The skull forms a tough and rigid protective covering around the brain.

10

Scientific research has shown that the human brain starts remembering things from the womb. The foetus' brain development commences an extraordinary journey from the moment of conception, that results in a highly developed brain.

11

There are about 100 billion tiny cells in our brains called 'neurons'. There are so many that it would take you over 3,000 years to count them all. Neurons develop at the rate of two hundred and fifty thousand per minute during the first trimester of pregnancy. A small piece of brain tissue, approximately 2mm in length, which is about the size of a grain of sand, contains approximately one hundred thousand neurons as well as one billion synapses.

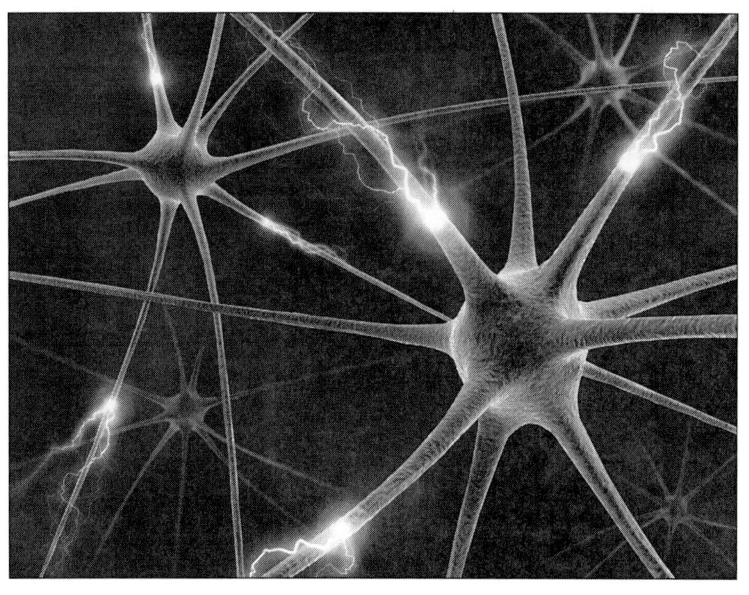

12

The human brain is made up of 60% percent white matter and 40% percent gray matter. Gray Matter is the darker tissue of the brain and spinal cord, is made up of neurons that gather and transmit information originating in the sensory organs or in other gray matter regions. White matter is a component of the central nervous system in the brain and the superficial spinal cord. It is made up of dendrites and axons, which create the network by which neurons send signals to the rest of the body.

13

It took 40 minutes for Supercomputer K to simulate just 1 second's worth of 1% of the activity of human brain. Despite advances in computing power, the human brain is still 30 times more powerful than the best supercomputers.

14

77-78% of our brain is just water, 10-12% lipids, 8% protein, 1% carbs, 2% soluble organics and 1% inorganic salts. So, if you get dehydrated by more than 2%, you can suffer from a loss of cognitive skills in memory.

15

Each minute, about 750 milliliters of blood travel through the brain.

16

It is currently impossible to measure the possible storage potential of a brain. A rough calculation by Paul Reber, Professor of Psychology at Northwestern University suggests that if a human brain was converted into a hard drive like device, it could store 2.5 Petabytes of data. That is 2,500,000 Gigabytes. Equals more than 500,000 DVDs or 100,000 blu ray disks.

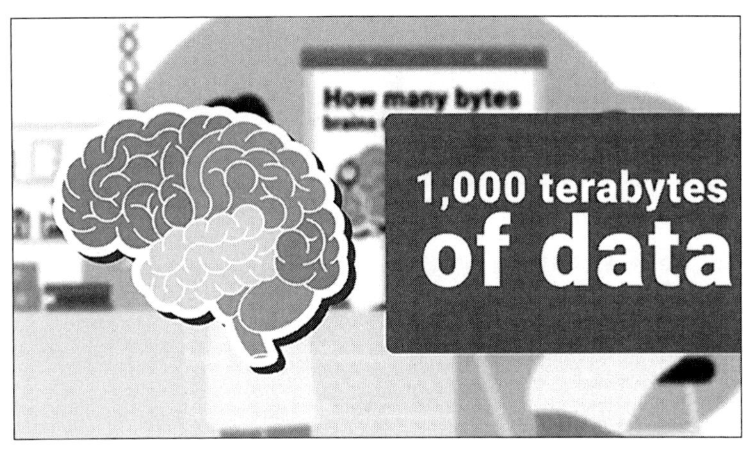

How many bytes
1,000 terabytes
of data

There are no pain receptors in the brain, so the brain can feel no pain. Nevertheless, what you feel during a headache is not your brain hurting. There are nociceptors in your head and neck that are capable of perceiving pain. These are the source of a headache.

18

The brain is the only object in the world that can contemplate itself.

19

The brain is the last part of your body to die. After you die, it continues to work for more than 10 minutes. Moments before death, your brain receives a surge of electricity. No one knows why it happens! It also begins to lose oxygen. Even when your heart beat stops, you are conscious for about 2-20 seconds. This is because the cerebral cortex can last without oxygen.

20

When a person is awake, his brain generates approximately 12-25 watts of electricity enough to power up a low watt bulb. More electrical impulses are generated in one day by a single human brain than by all the telephones in the world.

21

When your brain isn't focused on a task, it switches to a default mode. You can carry so many tasks almost instinctively because you have done it so many times. Your brain doesn't need to focus on it. So whenever it can, your brain will kick into this automatic decision—making gear to save energy, freeing up your conscious mind to work on other mentally taxing things. Interestingly, we are on this autopilot mode nearly half the time. Our autopilot mode seems to run by a set of brain structures called the default mode network, which is a constellation of different areas in your brain that work together, allowing our bodies to run on autopilot.

22

According to researchers, chronic stress changes your brain structure and functions which can lead to a multitude of mental problems. It increases the levels of a stress hormone called *cortisol*, affecting brain functions and putting you at risk for various mood disorders and mental issues such as depression and anxiety. High levels of stress hormones can stop the production of new brain cells in the part of your brain that stores memories, which can negatively affect your memory. When your head is full of stress, your brain can literally become inflamed.

anger
stress
sadness
failure
depression

23

Who do you think has a larger brain—modern humans or our early ancestors? This discovery surprised the researchers around the world. It turns out our 10,000 year old ancestors had larger brains than we do. About 10% larger to be exact. But it is not because they were necessarily smarter than us. Several neuroscientists have explained this change in brain size. Our brains are getting smaller because our bodies are too. So, that means we have a smaller nervous system, so we can afford to carry a lighter, more efficient brain than our ancestors.

 51 Must Know Facts About

24

Your brain stops growing when you are around 25, but that doesn't mean that you have reached your intellectual peak. Cognitive change is a lifelong process. Some skills like memory and processing speed max out at your 20's. You can excel at facial recognition and problem solving in your 30's and then gain emotional control and empathy in your 40's and 50's. A select few skills like vocabulary take even longer, peaking in your 60's and 70's. Now your brain may have matured but your mind has plenty of room to grow! That's why you should never stop learning no matter how old you get.

25

Have you ever heard that missing one of your senses amplifies the others? Going blind or losing your hearing gives you different neurological advantages. A 2011 study found that people who are born blind develop a new way to process the world around them. They essentially began seeing through their ears. The human brain excels at adapting to difficult situations; this kind of reorganisation is called *neuroplasticity*. So when someone can't see, the brain automatically searches for a new solution. It will often rewire itself to process auditory information over visual information. It isn't quite the same as normal vision. But this work around can yield some pretty amazing results.

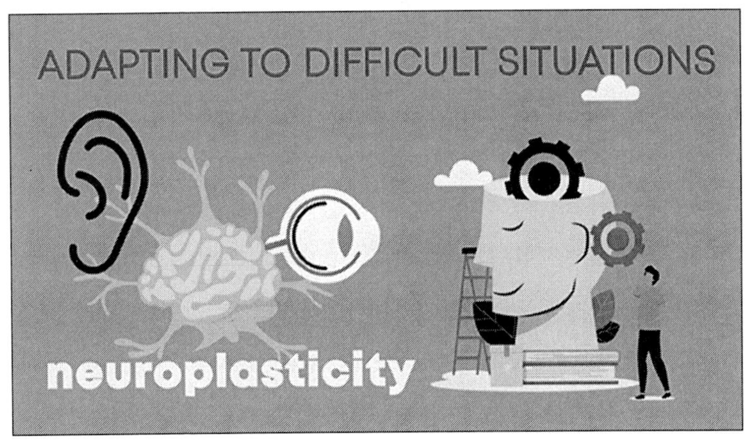

ADAPTING TO DIFFICULT SITUATIONS
neuroplasticity

26

The adult human brain weighs about 3 pounds (1,350g). It is about 2% of the total body weight. That's barely anything when you think about how important the brain is to your body. So how does such a small organ manage so many executive functions? The real difference between the brain and the rest of the body isn't in its size—it's the amount of oxygen and blood your brain needs to work like it's supposed to. Even though it's only 2% of your weight, it requires about 20% of your body's supply of oxygen. That's more than your entire skeletal muscles combine.

27

Since the brain needs so much blood, an intricate network of vessels is working around the clock to bring oxygen to every part of the brain. Because if one section isn't getting enough blood, you start losing basic functions. Some people experience blindness or fatigue, others lose all feelings or one or more parts of their body; almost like you are paralized. So, how many blood vessels does it take to keep your brain up and running? You would see that the average person has hundreds of miles of blood vessels inside his/her head. Your blood vessels are just so thin and tightly woven together, that they fit inside a much smaller space. Researchers are still working on counting the number of blood vessels inside the brain. However, we do know that the entire body measures upto 100,000 miles; that's like driving the widest part of the earth four times and those are the blood vessels of one average size person.

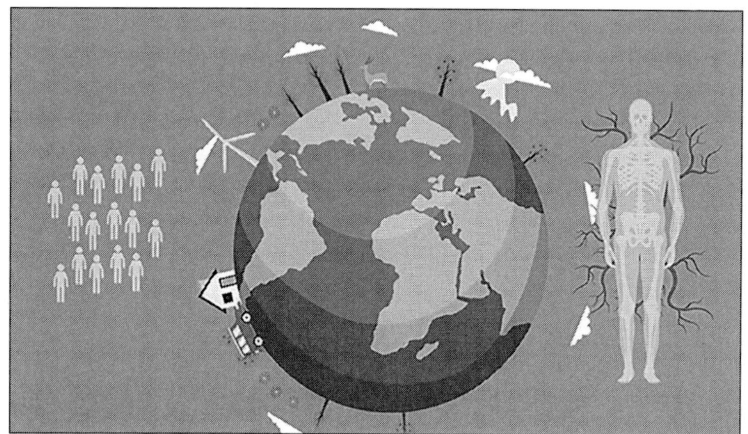

 51 Must Know Facts About

28

You spend the majority of the day thinking. So many random thoughts pop into your head all day long. But has anyone ever tried to count them? Researchers go back and forth on the exact number. But most agreed that the average person has about 50,000 thoughts every single day! That's at least 2,100 thoughts per hour. Most of them are short and repetitive. But this goes on to show that your brain never rests.

29

Every action in the brain starts with an electrical signal. Some are sluggish and slow. Others race across the brain clocking in over 230 miles per hour. The speed of a signal depends primarily on what kind of a signal it is. When you touch a hot surface for example, that sensation speeds through your body. It starts at the sensory receptors on your hand, passes through your spinal cord and then enters your cerebral cortex. There you perceive and process how hot the surface is, which sends a new electrical signal rushing through your brain and your body.

230 miles
per hour

30

Your brain is actually the fattiest organ inside your body. Think about the construction of your brain. Are you picturing the hundreds and millions of neurons? The complicated network of blood vessels. The dozens of glands secreting all kinds of hormones. But did you know that 60% of your brain is just plain fat? Despite being one of the largest organs in the body, your brain doesn't have any muscle. Your body makes a lot of different things, but fat isn't one of them. So, all the fat that your brain uses for performance and repair has to come from the food you eat. This is why so many dieticians push people to consume large amounts of omega-3 fatty acids. Now those important fats facilitate brain development, save off disease and preserve your mental health.

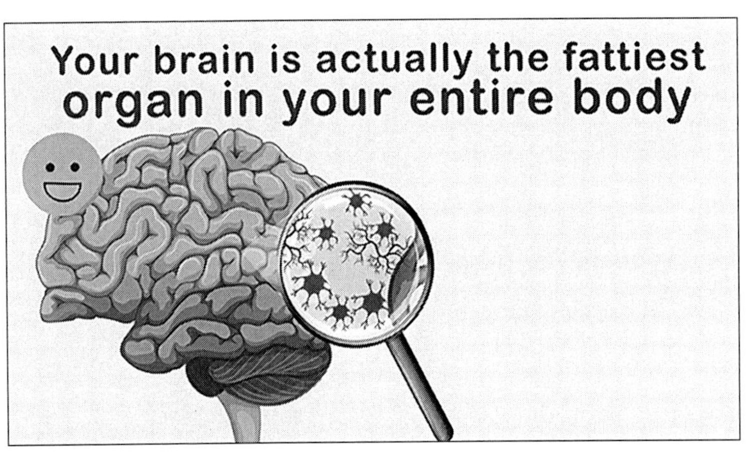

Your brain is actually the fattiest
organ in your entire body

31

The brain develops in a pretty strange way. When you are born, it is about one quarter of the size of an adult brain. This is pretty big considering how small an infant actually is. But as we all know, there are a lot of things the baby can't quite get their heads around. That's because their quarter sized brain is primarily focused on keeping them alive. The brain does not grow at a steady pace. It actually doubles in size during the first year of life. By 3 years old, your brain is almost 80% of an adult brain. That number jumps up to 90% by the age of 5. During those crucial years, your brain is forming millions of synapses every single second. It's learning everything from symbol recognition to behavioural habits, which are important functions that you'll need later in life.

32

When you see an image, it passes through your retina three times: firstly, as light to the receptor cells, secondly, as neural signals through the initial visual processing of the retina and thirdly, as neural signals via the optic nerve to the brain. All of these processes occur in thirteen milliseconds.

33

Have you ever wondered why you are unable to tickle yourself? The human brain can distinguish between an unexpected external touch and your own touch, this is the reason why you can't tickle yourself.

34

About 90 minutes after you fall asleep, you enter a stage called REM sleep. During this stage, your brain becomes highly active while your muscles become prayalyzed. Your breathing and heart rate becomes erratic. Your brain begins processing and recording information very actively, allowing you to remember what you have learned before sleeping. This is also when you start dreaming.

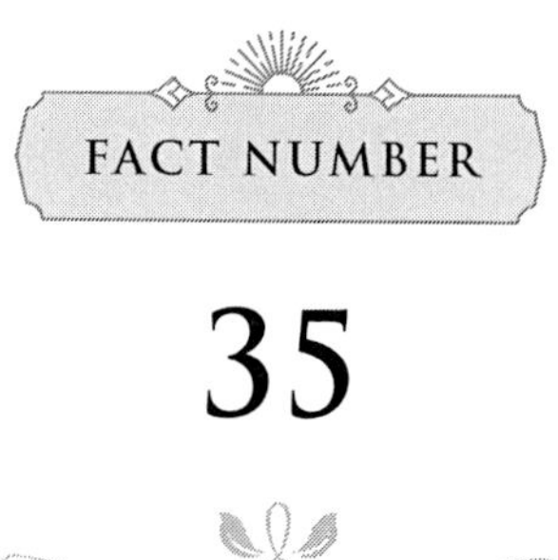

35

The ability of the brain to multitask is merely an illusion. According to the researchers, less than 3% of people can efficiently do two things simultaneously. For those of you who multitask on a regular basis, all your brain is doing is going back and forth from one task to another instantaneously, creating a semblance of multitasking.

36

The *amygdala* is recognized as a component of the limbic system and is thought to play a crucial role in processing emotions and behaviours. It has become best known for its role in fear processing. When we are exposed to a fearful stimulus, information about that stimulus is immediately sent to the *amygdala*, which can then send signals to areas of the brain like the hypothalamus to trigger a "fight or flight" response.

37

People find it hard to maintain eye contact when talking, possibly because the dual task of maintaining eye contact while also racking the brain for a word is just too demanding, so the brain pushes for breaking eye contact to focus exclusively on finding a word that will fulfil the obligation.

38

The reason we get more creative ideas in the shower
is because such relaxing activity triggers the brain to
release large amounts of *dopamine*. The more *dopamine*
that is released, the more creative we are. When we
have a relaxed state of mind, we are more likely to turn
attention inwards, able to make insightful connections.

39

It is a popular misconception that your brain records memories like a video. Instead, it takes snapshots of the more important pieces of the events and when you recall the event it simply guesses what happened in between based upon prior experience and generalisation

40

After the age of twenty-five or just when you reach peak development, the brain starts to slowly shrink. Research suggests that the male brain shrinks faster than the female brain.

41

Mirror neurons were discovered in the 1990's. It is now a growing belief of the scientific community that they are responsible for feelings of empathy. This is why when you see someone hurt himself or herself; the same pain area will light up in your brain causing you to flinch.

42

The brain is very poor at concentrating for long periods and needs to have a break approximately every 90 minutes.

43

With the exception of the various degenerative brain diseases, your brain never loses its ability to learn, change, and adapt to new situations. The brain is effectively plastic and is constantly rewiring itself depending upon the context.

44

Bacteria living in the gut can remotely influence the activity of cells in the brain. The food we eat influences the ability of bacteria in our gut to produce small molecules, some of which are capable of travelling all the way to the brain. These molecules affect the activity of cells in the brain that are involved in controlling inflammation and neurodegeneration.

45

The surgical world made its first real bit of progress in the late 18th century. Brain surgery is one of the most complicated and volatile kinds of surgery. Archaeologists found evidence that the first brain surgery happened during the stone age. Over 5,000 years ago, early humans were doing something called trepanation, it is when you remove a bone from someone's skull.

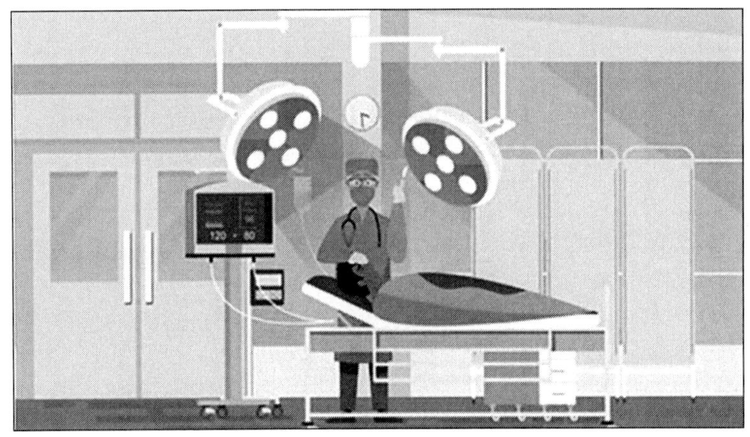

46

There are more than one hundred thousand chemical reactions happening in the brain every second.

47

When you embark on the process of learning something new or changing an old habit, you are essentially sending out positive emotions that come in the form of two hormones called *dopamine* and *serotonin*, which are released in the brain. *Dopamine* is a neurotransmitter that helps control the brain's pleasure or reward centres. *Serotonin* is a neurotransmitter, linked to tranquillity, reason, and calm. It keeps your emotions under control by helping with sleep and calming anxiety.

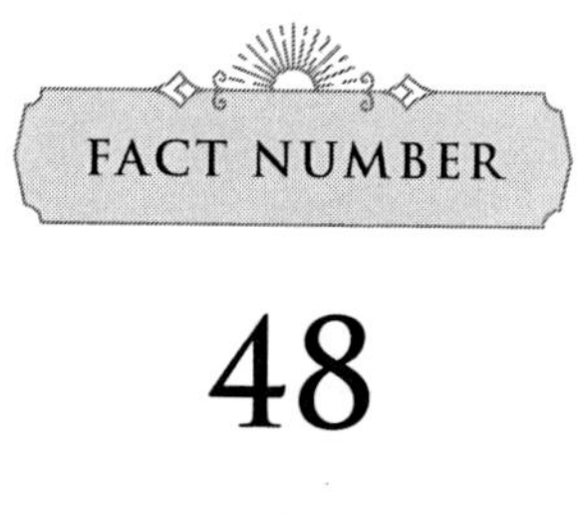

48

Ever wondered why we cry when we are extremely happy and extremely sad? A specific part of the limbic brain called the hypothalamus is highly involved in processing emotions and triggers crying as a response from intense emotions whether they are positive or negative.

49

Part of the reason why dieting is so difficult is also down to processes in your brain. When the body is deprived of food, neurons in the brain begin to cannibalize part of themselves, the process is known as *autophagy*, which literally means self eating. This provides a source of energy but also sets off hunger signals which prompt you to eat quickly.

50

Dreaming requires more brain activity than any waking function.

51

Your brain is constantly working to maintain a sense of continuity in your vision and perception of time, but even the slightest movement of eyes can disrupt this. Whenever you quickly move your eyes from one point of focus to another, there is a tiny disruption in your vision, which your brain fills in by forcing you to perceive the new visual scene for a split longer. This is why when you first look at an analogue clock, it appears as though the second hand takes a moment longer than a second to move.

OTHER BOOKS YOU MAY LIKE

- 1984 by George Orwell, ISBN: 9789380914947
- 12 Years a Slave by Solomon Northup, ISBN: 9789390492374
- 51 Most Powerful Prayers by Ryan, ISBN: 9789354990847
- A Christmas Carol by Charles Dickens, ISBN: 9788193545874
- A Cloud by Day, a Fire by Night by AW Tozer, ISBN: 9789354990854
- A Passage to India by E.M. Forster, ISBN: 9789354990205
- A Room of One's Own by Virginia Woolf, ISBN: 9789354990281
- A Streetcar Named Desire by Tennessee Williams, ISBN: 9788194748601
- A Wrinkle in Time by Madeleine L'Engle, ISBN: 9789354991066
- Abraham Lincoln by Lord Charnwood, ISBN: 9789380914251
- Absolute Surrender by Andrew Murray, ISBN: 9789389716269
- Animal Farm by George Orwell, ISBN: 9789380914701
- Anthem by Ayn Rand, ISBN: 9789389157079
- As a Man Thinketh by James Allen, ISBN: 9788180320262
- As I Lay Dying by William Faulkner, ISBN: 9789390492381
- Awakened Imagination by Neville Goddard, ISBN: 9789389157086
- Be What You Wish by Neville Goddard, ISBN: 9789387669550
- Chanakya Neeti by Chanakya, ISBN: 9789389716276
- Civilization and Its Discontents by Sigmund Freud, ISBN: 9789387669499
- Delighting in God by AW Tozer, ISBN: 9788194748632
- Demian by Hermann Hesse, ISBN: 9789387669567
- Experiencing the Holy Spirit by Andrew Murray, ISBN: 9788194764809
- Feeling is the Secret by Neville Goddard, ISBN: 9789389157109
- George Orwell Combo : Animal Farm & 1984, ISBN: 9789390492459
- Gravity by George Gamow, ISBN: 9789388118484
- Guerrilla Warfare by Ernesto Che Guevara, ISBN: 9789354990366

Develop your reading habit | **Gift books to your friends**

OTHER BOOKS YOU MAY LIKE

- How to be filled with the Holy Spirit by AW Tozer, ISBN: 9789389157116
- How to Develop Self Confidence by Dale Carnegie, ISBN: 9789387669000
- In His Steps by Charles M. Sheldon, ISBN: 9789390492794
- Life of Christ by Fulton J. Sheen, ISBN: 9789389716306
- Lost Horizon by James Hilton, ISBN: 9789389716313
- Man: The Dwelling Place of God by AW Tozer, ISBN: 9789354990656
- Maneaters of Kumaon by Jim Corbett, ISBN: 9789354990731
- Mansarover 1 (Hindi) by Premchand, ISBN: 9789380914978
- Mansarover 2 (Hindi) by Premchand, ISBN: 9789380914985
- Meditation and Its Methods by Swami Vivekananda, ISBN: 9789389716320
- One, None and a Hundred Thousand by Luigi Pirandello, ISBN: 9789389716337
- Paths to Power by AW Tozer, ISBN: Forthcoming
- Scientific Healing Affirmations by P. Yogananda, ISBN: 9789389716344
- Selected Stories of Rabindranath Tagore by Tagore, ISBN: 9789380914770
- Siddhartha by Hermann Hesse, ISBN: 9789380914145
- Student's Encyclopedia of G. K. by GP Editors, ISBN: 9789380914190
- Tales from Shakespeare by Charles Lamb & Mary Lamb, ISBN: 9789380914367
- The Alchemy of Happiness by Al-Ghazzali, ISBN: 9789387669505
- The Book of Enoch by Enoch, ISBN: 9789390492480
- The Dynamic Laws of Prosperity by Catherine Ponder, ISBN: 9789388118156
- The Game of Life and How to Play It by Florence Shinn, ISBN: 9789387669390
- The Imitation of Christ by Thomas À Kempis, ISBN: 9789388118057
- The Knowledge of the Holy by AW Tozer, ISBN: 9789389157130
- The Law by Neville Goddard, ISBN: 9789390492886
- The Light of Asia by Sir Edwin Arnold, ISBN: 9789380914923
- The Magic of Believing by Claudie Bristol, ISBN: 9789388118149

Develop your reading habit | **Gift books to your friends**